# THE SAW

## LEARNING ABOUT TOOLS

David and Patricia Armentrout

The Rourke Book Co., Inc.
Vero Beach, Florida 32964

PHOTO CREDITS
©Sears, Roebuck and Co.: cover; Stanley Tools: title, page 15;
© Armentrout: page 4; © East Coast Studios: pages 12, 17; © Black &
Decker: pages 10, 18, 21; © Shopsmith: pages 7, 8; © Fine
Woodworking Magazine: page 13

**Library of Congress Cataloging-in-Publication Data**

Armentrout, Patricia, 1960-
    The saw / by Patricia Armentrout and David Armentrout.
        p.  cm. — (Learning about tools)
    Includes index.
    ISBN 1-55916-122-1
    1. Saws—Juvenile literature.    [1. Saws.  2. Tools.]
I. Armentrout, David, 1962-  II. Title  III. Series.
TJ1233.A76  1995
621.9' 3—dc20                                              94–46475
                                                            CIP
                                                            AC

**Printed in the USA**

# TABLE OF CONTENTS

# THE SAW

There are many types of tools. Some tools are used for pounding or drilling, while others are used for cutting and shaping. One of the most useful cutting tools is the saw.

As with most tools, saws are made in various shapes and sizes. Different types of saws are used to cut through wood, metal, and other materials.

*Loggers use chain saws to cut
down trees and split large logs*

## THE BLADE

Most saws have a cutting edge called the blade. Saw blades are made of metal and have one or more rows of sharp teeth, or points.

The teeth, or points, can vary in number depending on the type of saw.

Saws with many small points, spaced close together, leave a smooth cut edge. Saws that have fewer and larger points leave a rough edge.

*The blade on this coping saw will leave a smooth cut edge*

# LUMBER

Saws play an important part in the lumber **industry** (IN-dus-tree). They are used to cut logs before the logs are sold to lumber yards or stores.

Trees are first cut with large power saws and taken to a sawmill by truck or train. The logs are stripped of their bark and cut with a headsaw to square them off.

The squared logs are cut into boards, or lumber. Finally, the boards are cut into different lengths and widths and are shipped out for sale.

*Lumber yards and hardware stores offer a wide variety of lumber from which to choose*

## PEOPLE WHO USE SAWS

Loggers, carpenters, and many construction workers use saws. Cutting and shaping any hard material would be very hard to do without a saw!

Woodworkers use saws to help construct big buildings, houses, and furniture.

Even plumbers need to use saws. Many pipes are made of hard plastic. These pipes need to be cut in length before fitting in small spaces, like under kitchen sinks.

*While cutting pipe, a plumber wears safety glasses to protect his eyes*

*A line drawn on a piece of wood is used as a guide for cutting*

*A coping saw is commonly used to cut curves and to cut around small corners*

## BASIC SAWS

Two basic handsaws used in woodworking are the crosscut saw and the ripsaw.

The crosscut saw is the most common. It is used to cut *against* wood grain and will produce a clean cut. Many home craftsmen own a crosscut saw.

The ripsaw is used to cut *with* wood grain. The cut produced by the teeth is **coarse** (kors), or rough, because the teeth chip, or rip, away the wood.

*A carpenter uses a crosscut saw to cut lumber down to size*

## METAL AND GLASS CUTTERS

The hacksaw is popular for cutting many types of metals. A hacksaw blade with fine, or small, teeth is used to cut thin pieces of metal. Thick metals, such as iron or steel, should be cut with a blade that has large, coarse teeth.

Cutting glass or ceramic tile takes a special type of blade. The blade is called a grit-edge rod. This type of blade is made of thousands of **particles** (PAR-tik-ulz) called **tungsten carbide** (TUNG-sten) (KAR-bide). Tungsten carbide is a strong, hard man-made material.

*Cutting a metal rod is simple when using a hacksaw*

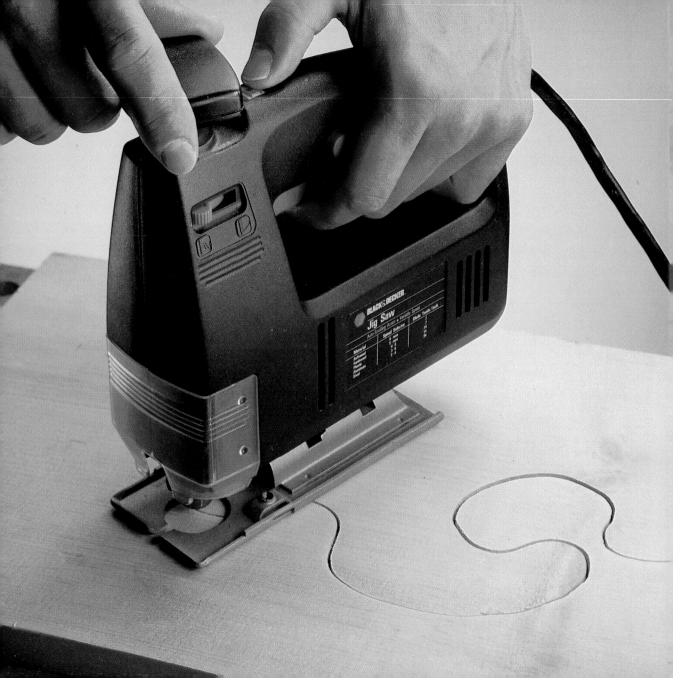

## SABER SAWS

A saber saw, or jigsaw, is a **portable** (PORT-a-bul) electric saw. It is easy to use and can be guided with one hand.

The saber saw can do the job of many other saws, such as the crosscut saw and hacksaw. The wide selection of blades that fit a saber saw make it possible to cut metals, plastics and woods.

Many home craftsmen own a saber saw because it is so **versatile** (VER-sa-tile).

*A jigsaw can be used to cut many shapes, even curves and circles!*

# TABLE SAWS

The table saw is an electric powered saw. A sturdy table supports a round, flat saw blade that juts out of the table's surface.

Instead of sawing through a piece of **stationary** (STAY-shun-ary) wood, the user guides the wood across the table top towards the moving blade.

A special feature of the table saw is the blade guard. It covers most of the blade while the saw is in use. This guard helps to protect hands and fingers from injury.

*Blade guards protect carpenters from accidental injury*

# CHAIN SAWS

Years ago those working in the logging industry were the main users of the chain saw. Today, home craftsmen as well as loggers make use of the powerful saw.

Farmers use the chain saw to clear trees from their land. Builders use the saw to construct log homes. Homeowners cut logs for their fireplace or trim dead limbs from backyard trees.

Chain saws come in small and large models and have gas or electric powered motors.

## Glossary

**coarse** (kors) — rough or harsh

**industry** (IN-dus-tree) — a business or trade as a whole

**particles** (PAR-tik-ulz) — very small pieces

**portable** (PORT-a-bul) — easily moved or carried

**stationary** (STAY-shun-ary) — fixed in a certain place or position, not moving

**tungsten carbide** (TUNG-sten) (KAR- bide) — a hard, man-made material made of metal and carbon

**versatile** (VER-sa-tile) — having many uses

# INDEX